**Welcome to the
'Highly Tooned World'
of
Rallying**

Rallyist-2

Cartoons by
Paul M. Ellender

A Rallyist Publication

First Edition: Launched October 2010
Published by Rallyist Publications
Produced & Edited by Paul M. Ellender

ISBN 978-0-9562214-1-4

Printed by
Mixam UK Ltd
Watford
ENGLAND

Rallyist Publications.
Leyland
Lancashire
United Kingdom

Th'Artist

Apparently, I can't draw Horses, unlike my Father or my Uncle Vic. Not my fault, it's just I've never felt the need. Not that I've anything against Horses you understand, my interest has always focused on Horsepower. A former Formula Ford 1600, Vauxhall Chevette and Alfasud Prod-Saloon Racing Driver, I have always fostered a passion for motor sport.

My connection to Rallying however came not from the curious Racing Lines I could adopt navigating a route through the corners of the Racing Circuits of Britain, or even my ability to still control the car when driving next to the track rather than on it. My association came via membership with The Clitheroe and District Motor Club, participating as Event and Sector Marshall. This activity introduced me to the people and characters of the Rallying world and ultimately the humour. From this, the humour was soon converted into cartoon form for the then Club Newsletter 'Wrongslot'.

Rallyist is now one year old, and from that very, very wet weekend at Chatsworth's 2009 Rallyshow, the Rallyist Publications trade stand has visited many great events, and venues around England even jumping over the board to Scotland. The feed back for 'The Rallyist' from my many visitors has been fantastic, with requests for art work in other formats ultimately leading to the new range of Rallyist Merchandise, New potential Titles, and lots more material.

Thankyou for your support...

Paul Mc Ellend

To
Bill Asprey

&

Cartoon-World
www.cartoonworld.org

"For Opening That First Door..."

My Thanks

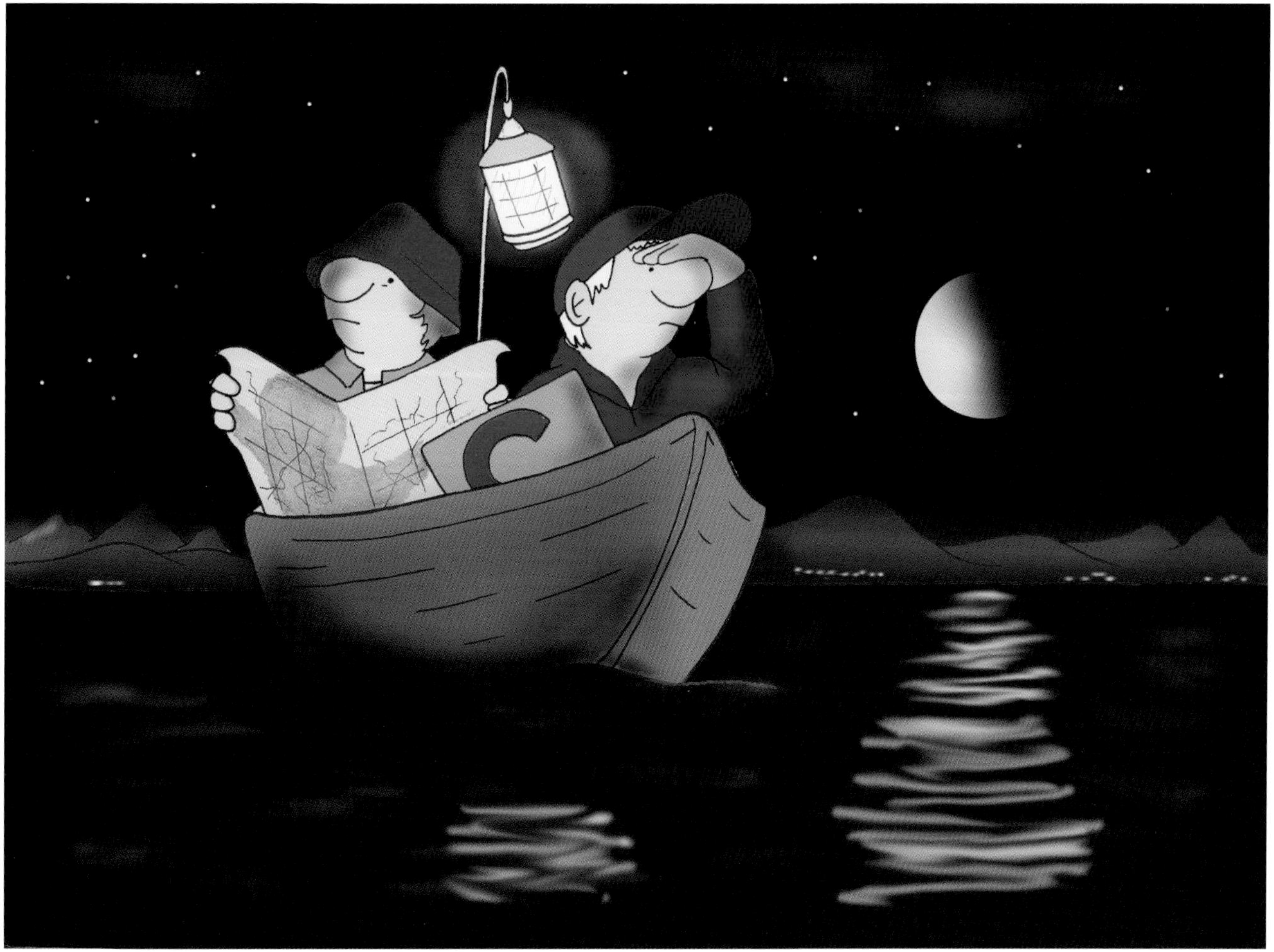
C

This can't be TC 5

Paul M Elleno

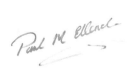

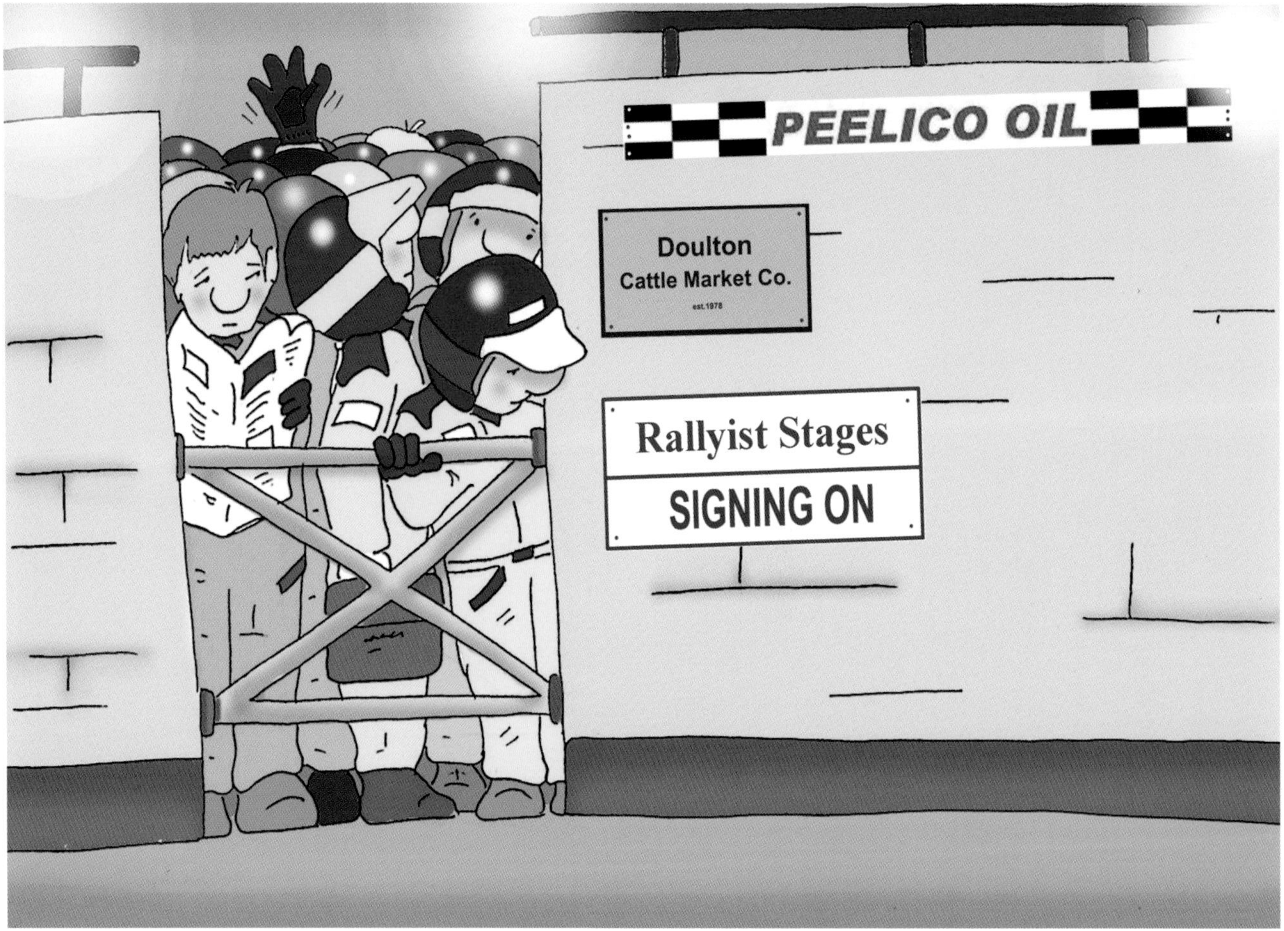
PEELICO OIL
Doulton
Cattle Market Co.
est.1978
Rallyist Stages
SIGNING ON

I was thinking more along the lines of Pace Notes
To help get a feel for the Island...

Focused? I'll say, nothing distracts my Lads on Rally day.

Well I'll tell you this....If he ends up on his roof
I'm not going in after him..

Look I honestly thought the Paradise Isle Rally
was the Venue.

I think the Bungies may have been
a mistake.

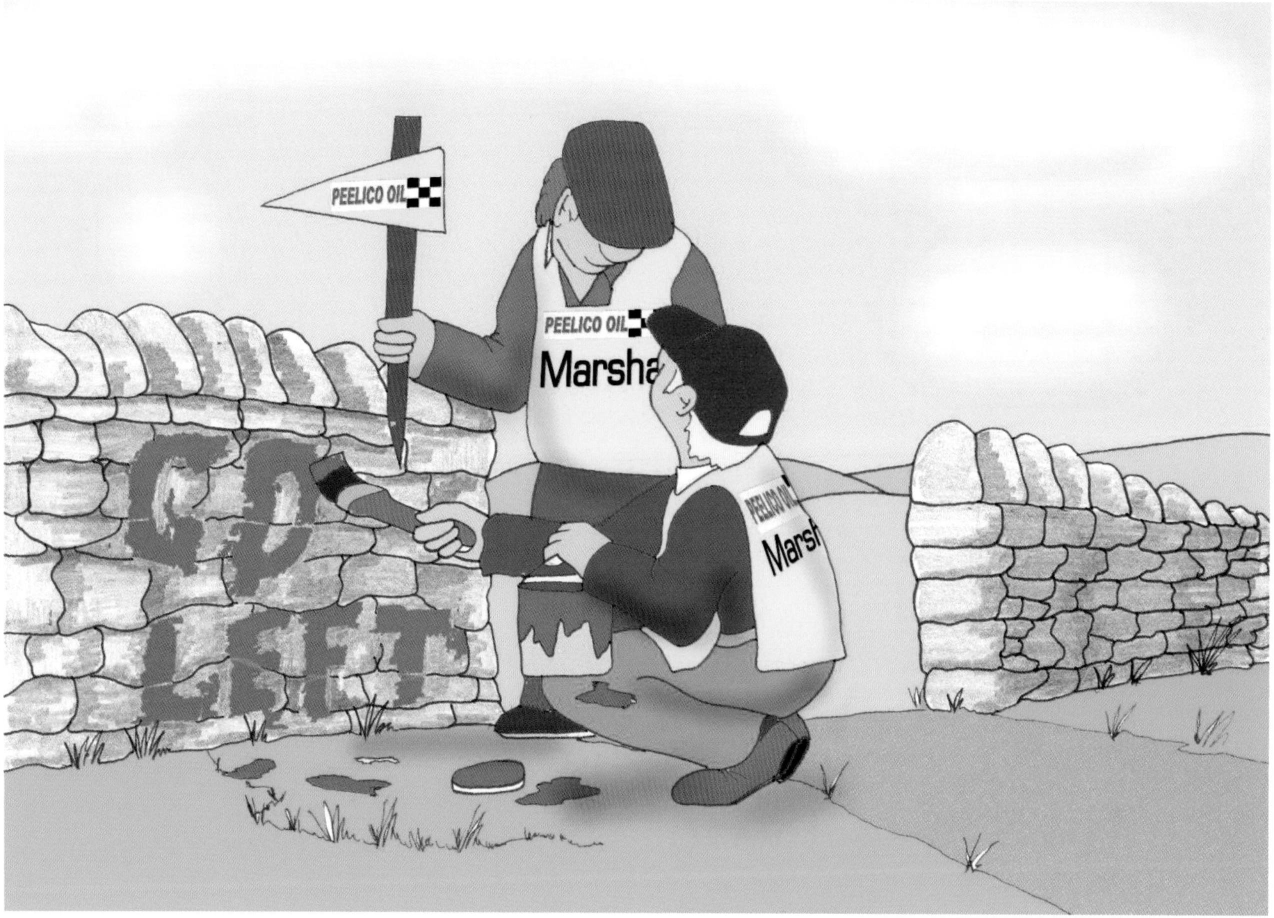
PEELICO OIL
PEELICO OIL
Marsha
PEELICO OIL
Marsh

We prefer to use these....

Paul M Ellenel

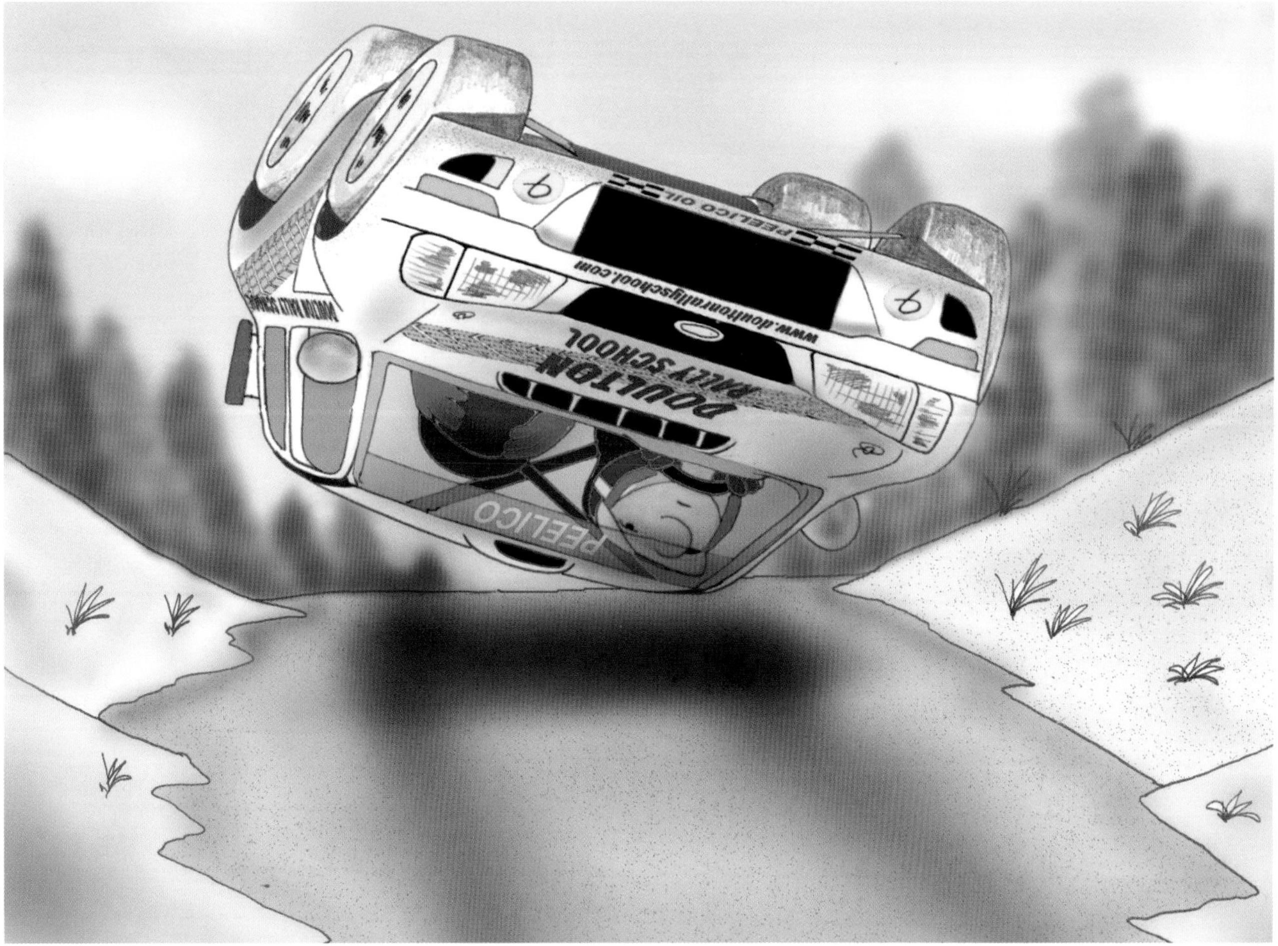
PEELICO OIL
www.doultonrallyschool.com
DOULTON RALLY SCHOOL
PEELICO

What should I do now?

I don't care what you used to do at
Donnington Park
Don't Kerb Hop Here!

Think perhaps your Dad
may have missed the point about a
Works Drive?

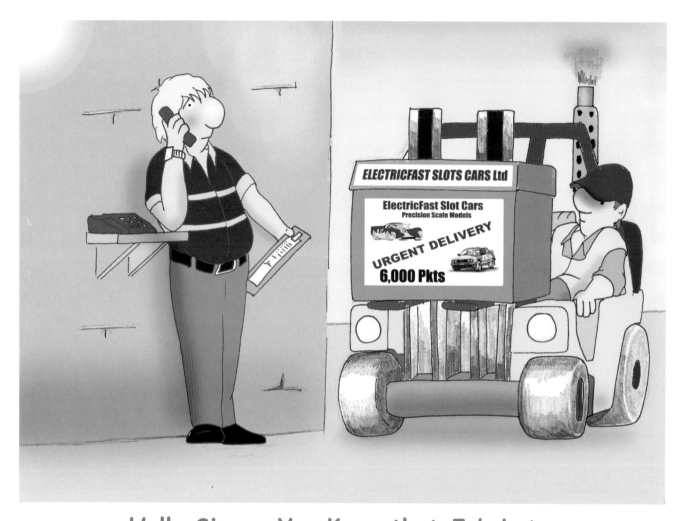

Hello Simon, You Know that Job Lot
of Rally Tyres you Bought on the Web

You don't think we may have over done the Bales?

I'm all for advantage Pete.
But this is a little over the top
even for Tarmac Events.

I think calling it a Launch,
May have been a Mistake

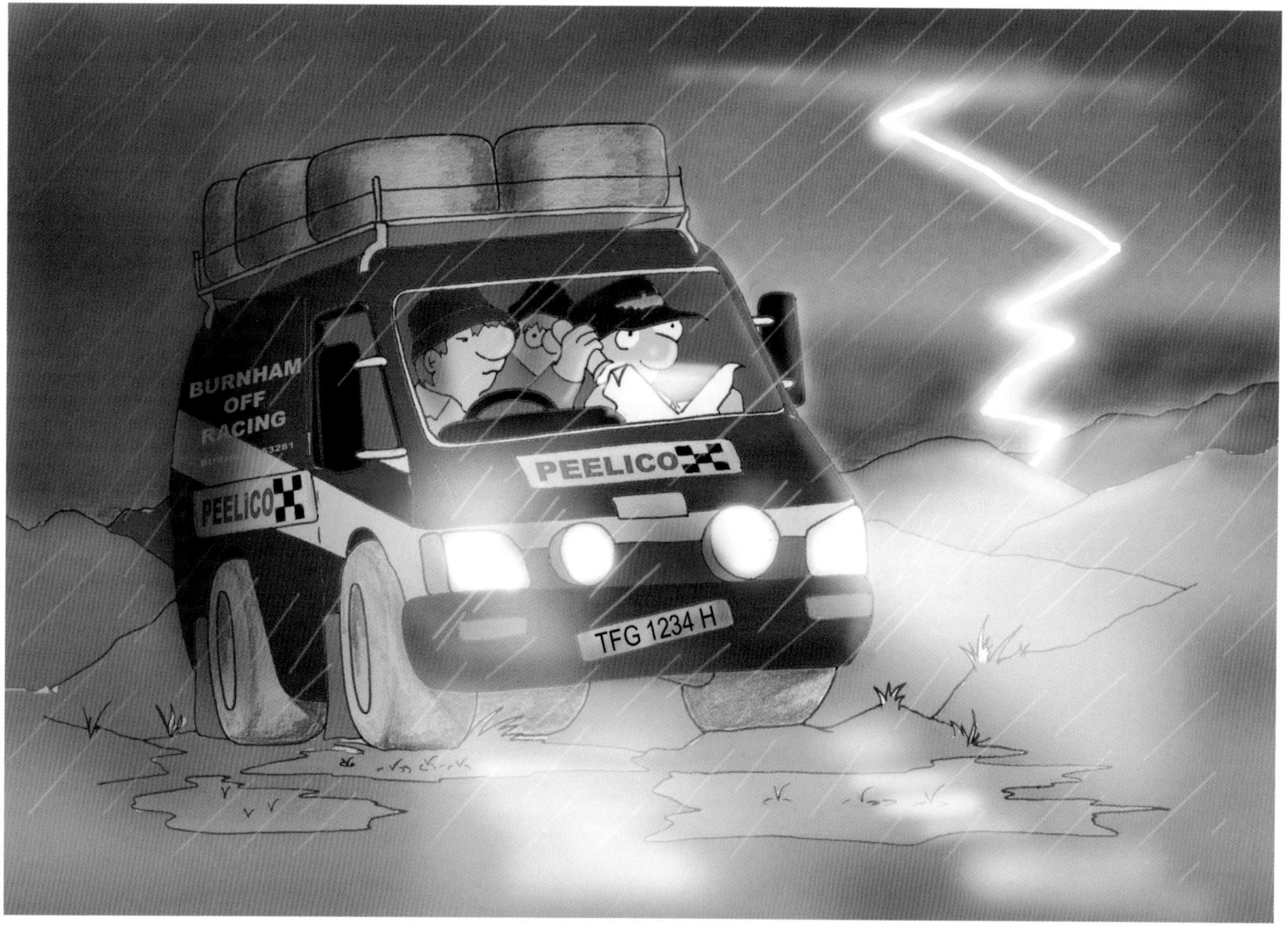
BURNHAM
OFF
RACING
PEELICO
PEELICO
TFG 1234 H

You know once, the Wife actually wanted me to go shopping on a night like this.

Paul M Ellen

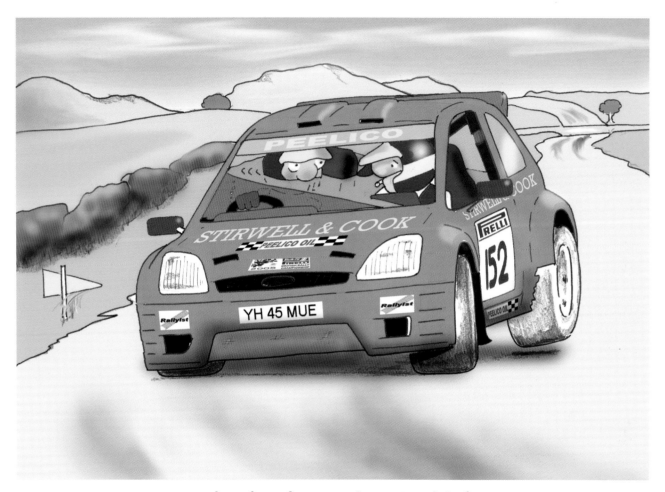

I think those Drain Holes
have Silted up again...

"If I could just find some sort of Reference Point..."

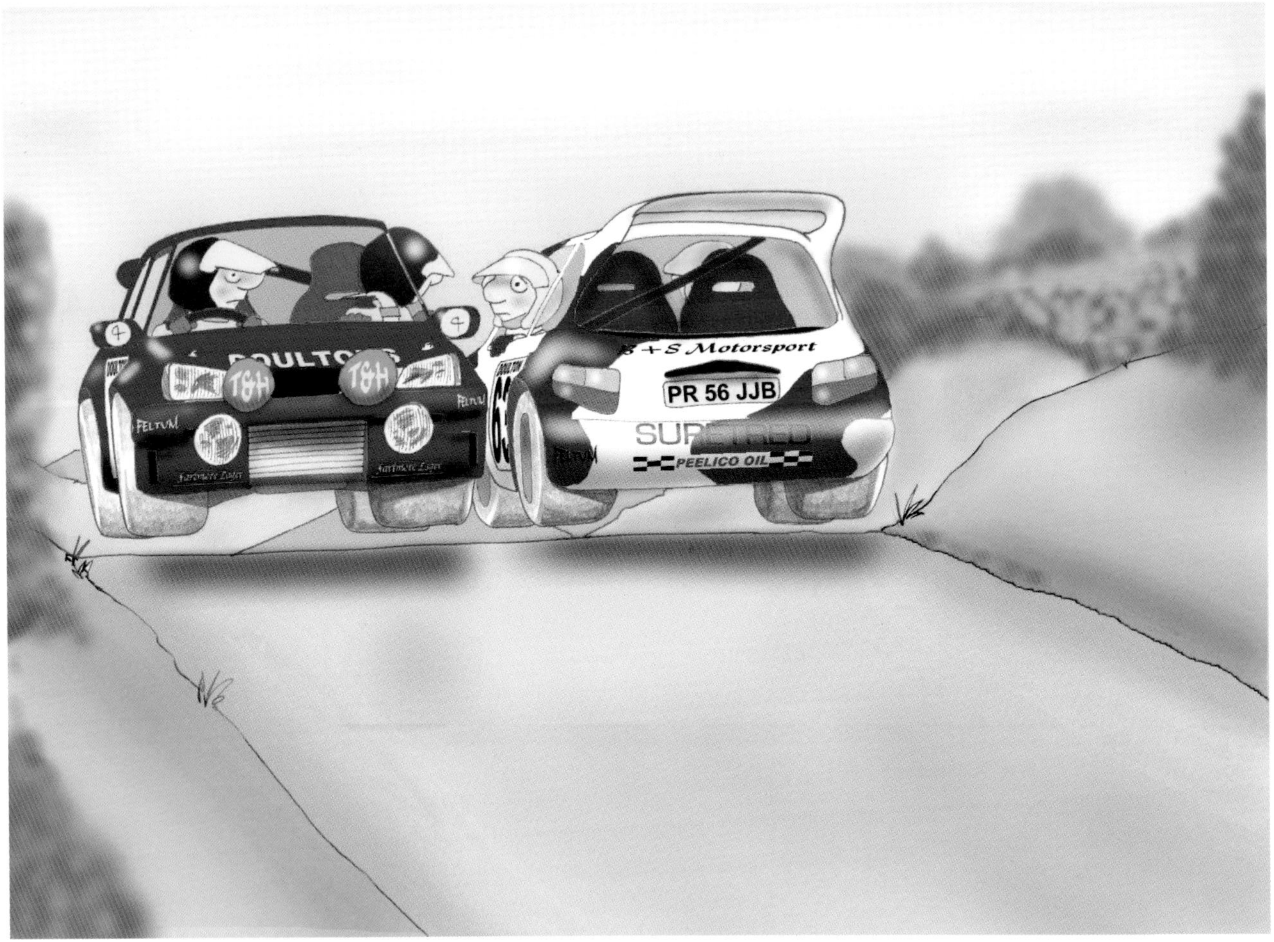
B + S Motorsport
PR 56 JJB
PEELICO OIL
FELTUM
T&H
T&H

Well that was a dumb place to Stop!

A push would have done, Lads

Read that last bit again!

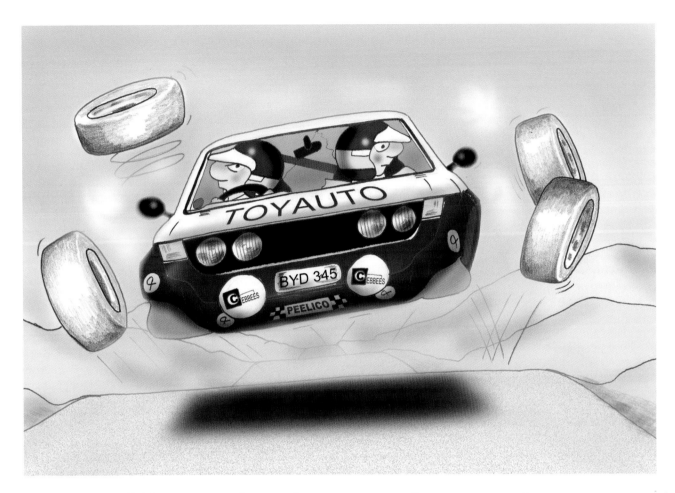

OK, So what have you been saying
to the Crew this time?

There you are,
I said the Tyres had gone off!

Apparently some guy called Robert the Bruce
came through here in 13:23
Wow, it must have been an Old Group 'B'

I think we should have gone over that Bridge
you know....

What he should have done was let the tail drift,
then brake, before powering through the banking,
Works for me in th'old van.

Honest I thought this Blue line was a
Motorway..

Stupid place to leave them anyway.

If we must see another WRC event
Lets do Cyprus

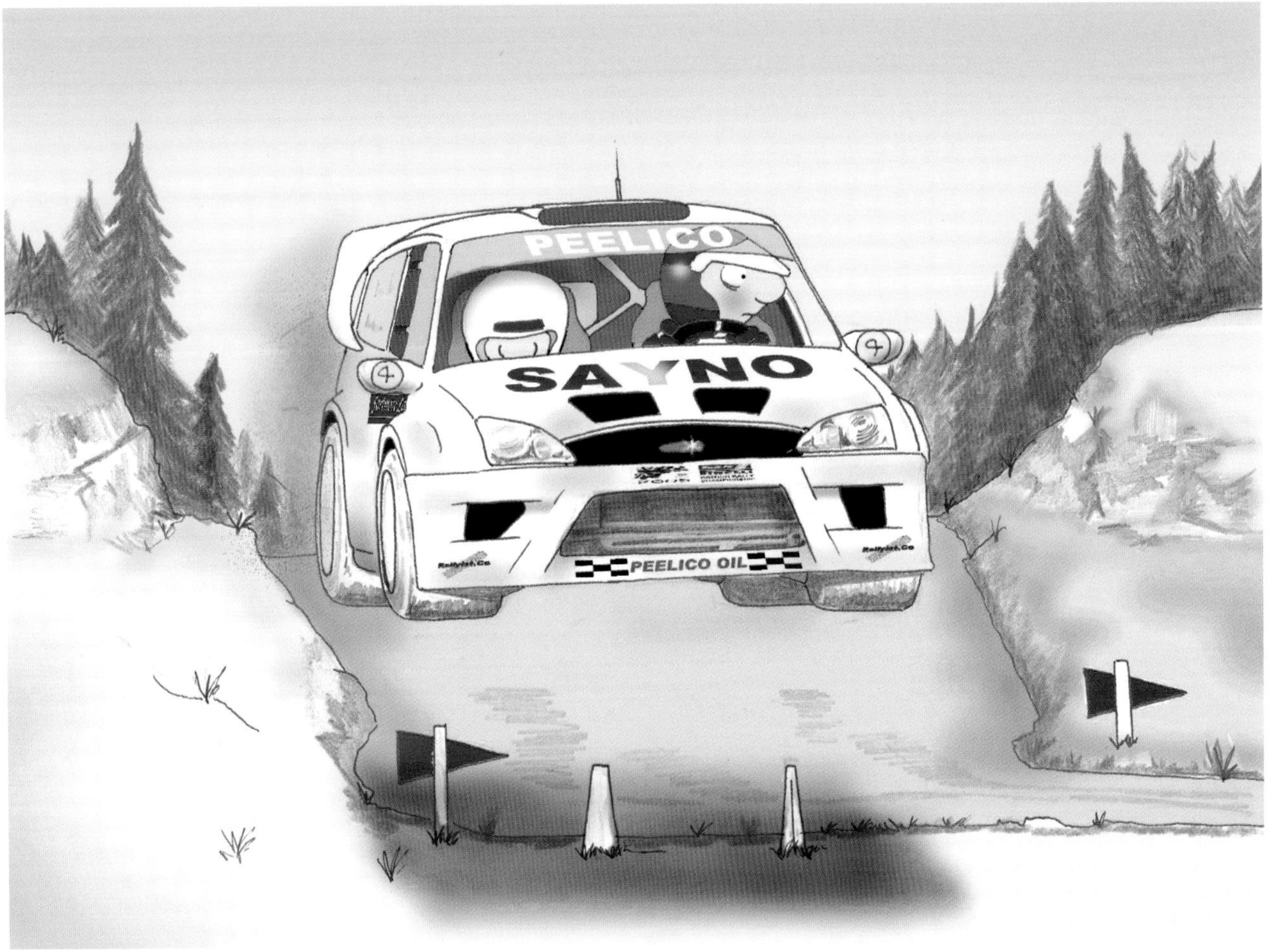
PEELICO
SAYNO
4
PEELICO OIL

Well I can only put so much detail in the Pace Notes...

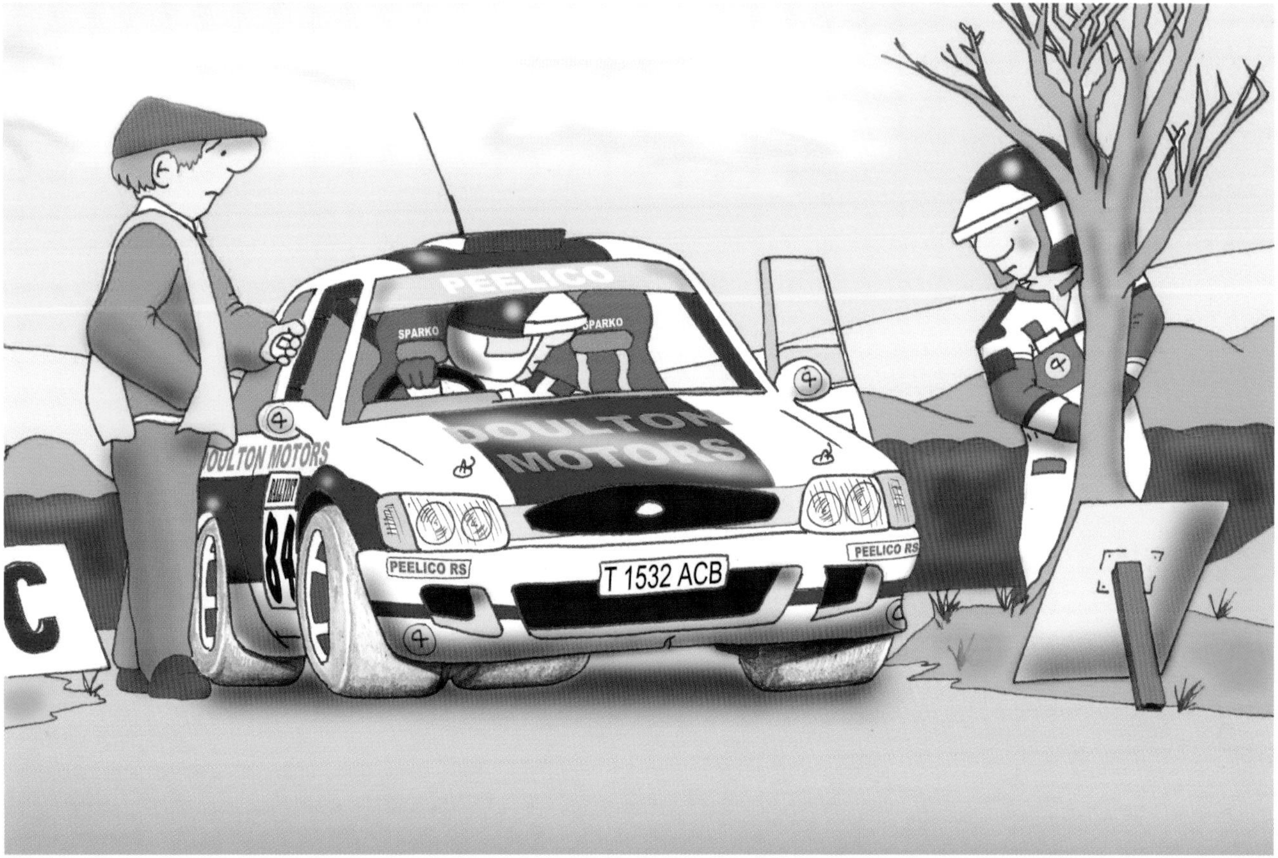
PEELICO
SPARKO
SPARKO
DOULTON MOTORS
DOULTON MOTORS
84
PEELICO RS
PEELICO RS
T 1532 ACB
C

Paul M Elland

Looks like we may have found a good spot.

I wondered if we could perhaps do the link somewhere else?

Look John, if we're late, we're late

Jeff found some screws rolling around the floor on your side earlier. Keep an eye out out for...!

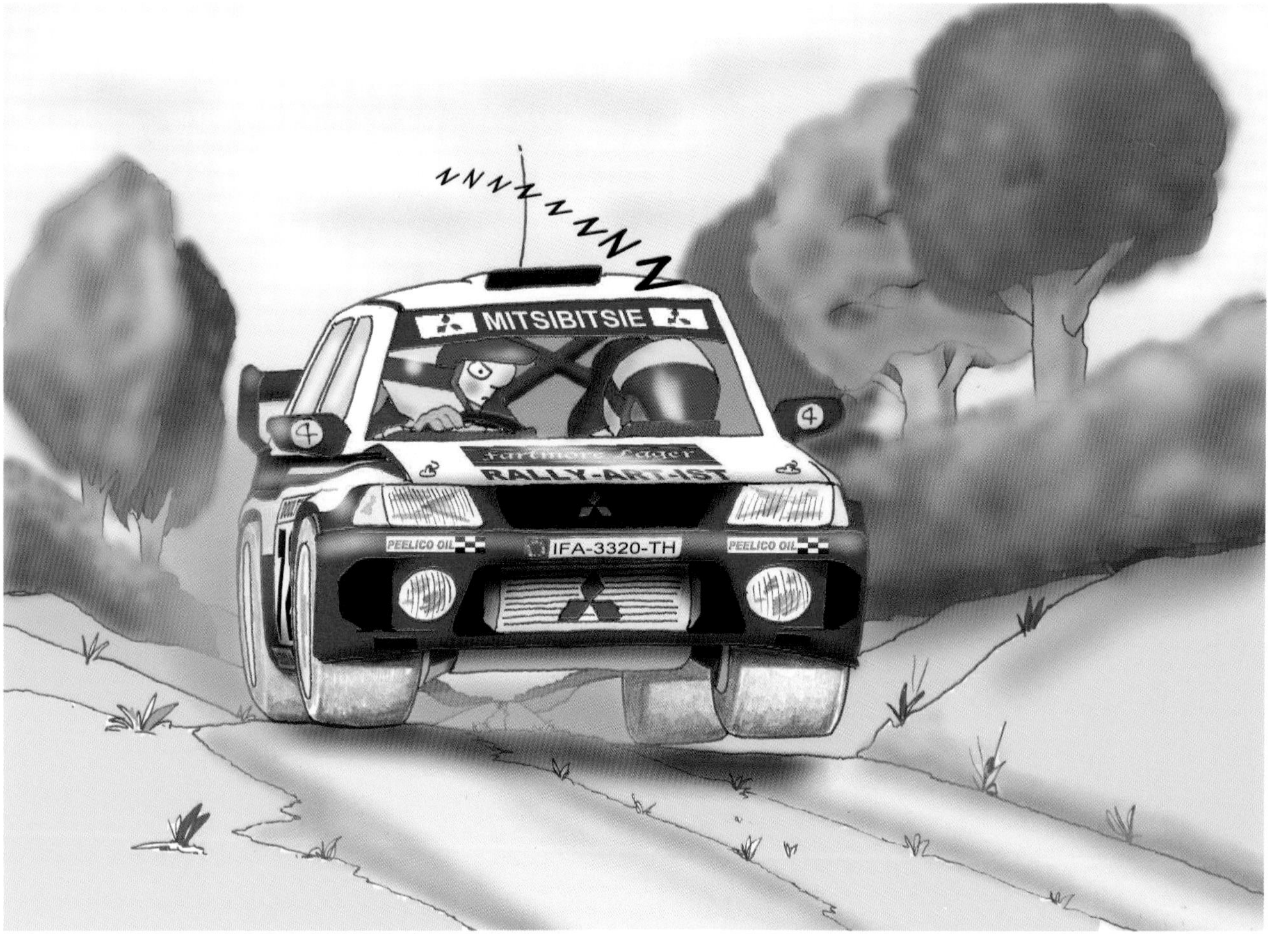
MITSIBITSIE
Fartmore Lager
RALLY-ART-IST
PEELICO OIL
IFA-3320-TH
PEELICO OIL

For Gods sake...Its only a Wasp!

You never see these F1 Chaps doing this..

Do you really have to burst into
'Help Me Rhonda' everytime we see a Sign?

Well now we know that noise wasn't
a faulty Wheel Bearing

Houston....We have a problem!

Oh Yes, I want to review the Suspension
settings before we leave for Germany OK?

We must be doing well
Everybody is waving at us!

If you say, its a good job its not a new one,
just one more time...

Do you think we'll have enough car
to get to the end of the Rally?

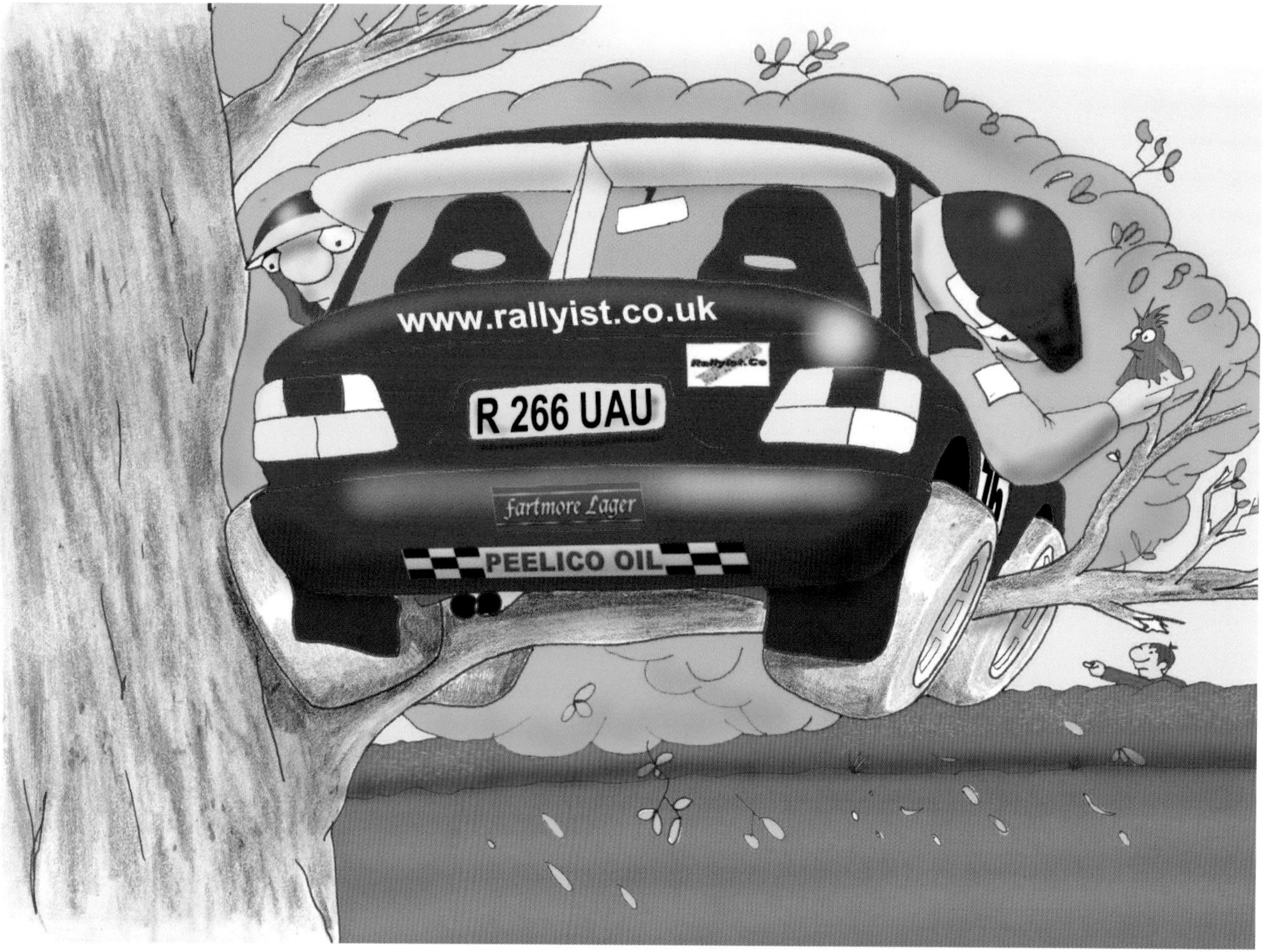
www.rallyist.co.uk
Rallyist.Co
R 266 UAU
Fartmore Lager
PEELICO OIL

Now just remind me again,
We do this for Fun....Yes?

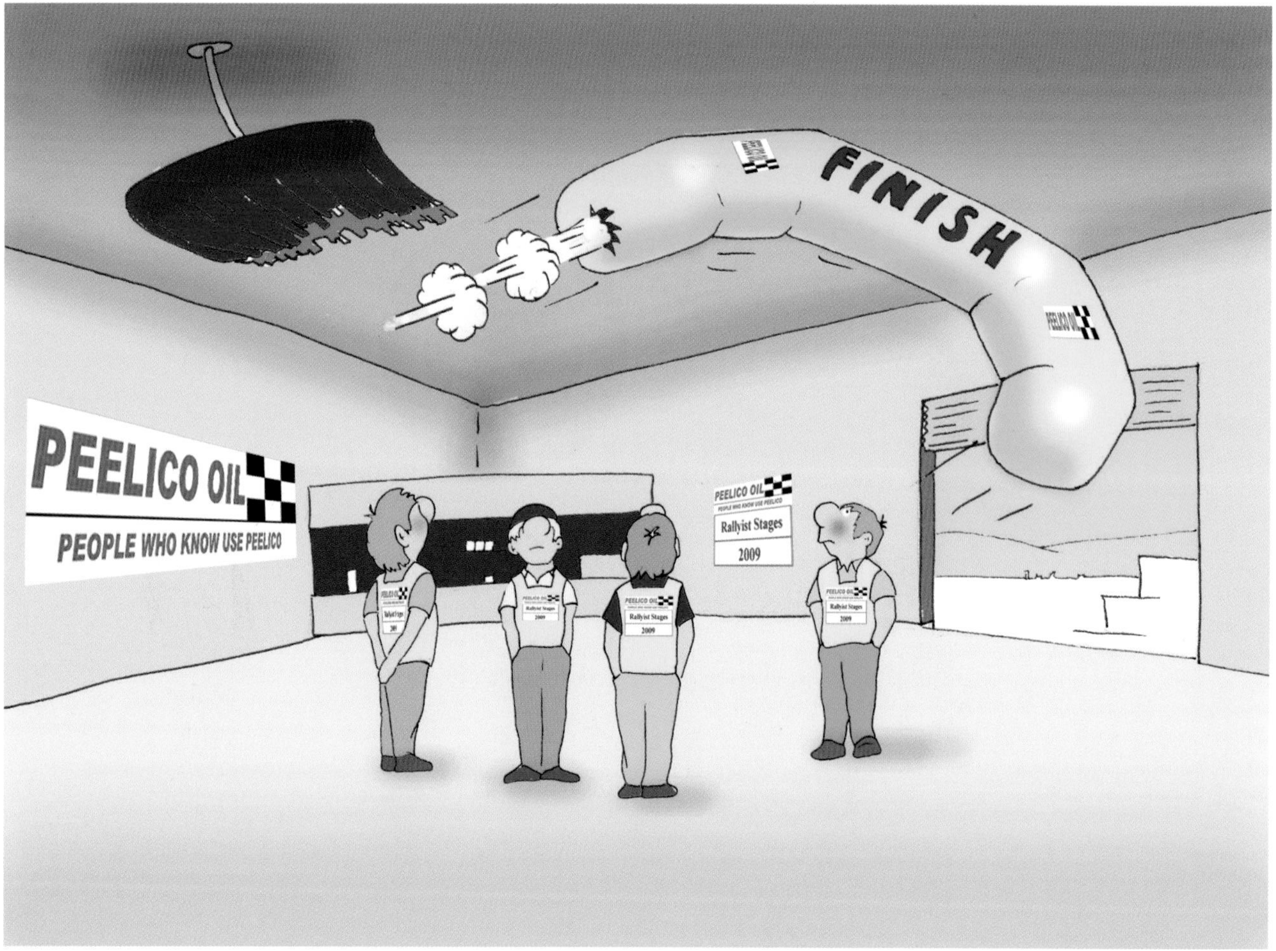
FINISH
PEELICO OIL
PEOPLE WHO KNOW USE PEELICO
PEELICO OIL
PEOPLE WHO KNOW USE PEELICO
Rallyist Stages
2009

"Oh Bollocks!"

Special Thanks;

The Tackle and Books, Tobermory, The Island of Mull
North West Stages 2010
John Leahy www.theandrewsyears.co.uk

****

Other Titles From Paul M. Ellender.

The Rallyist
Rallyist-2

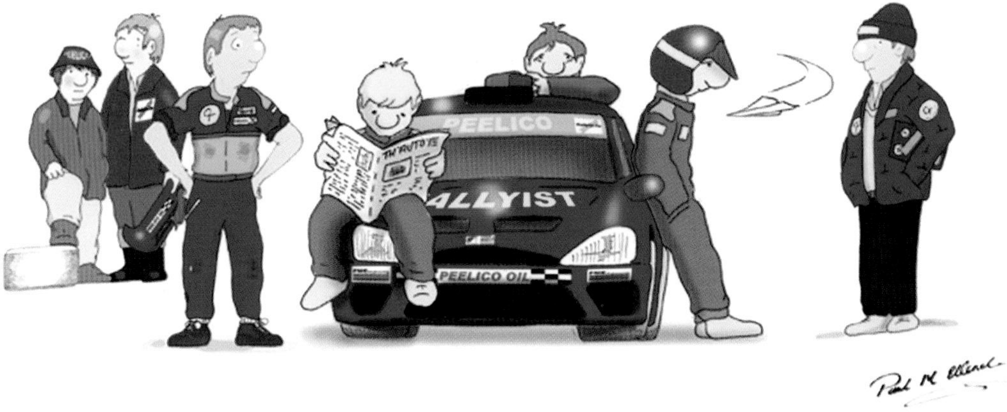
PEELICO
ALLYIST
PEELICO OIL

Watch out for more great Titles in the future from Rallyist Publications

"So What's Coming Next?

"Too Much Speed, Not Enough Track"

**Following in the Tyre Tracks of
The Rallyist & The Rallyist-2
The Rallyist goes Racing,
Focusing this Time, on the equally 'Highly Tooned' World
of Motor Racing**